IF FOUND PLEASE RETURN TO:

D1641017

Greater Than a Tourist Book Series
Reviews from Readers

I think the series is wonderful and beneficial for tourists to get information before visiting the city.

-Seckin Zumbul, Izmir Turkey

I am a world traveler who has read many trip guides but this one really made a difference for me. I would call it a heartfelt creation of a local guide expert instead of just a guide.

-Susy, Isla Holbox, Mexico

New to the area like me, this is a must have!

-Joe, Bloomington, USA

This is a good series that gets down to it when looking for things to do at your destination without having to read a novel for just a few ideas.

-Rachel, Monterey, USA

Good information to have to plan my trip to this destination.

-Pennie Farrell, Mexico

Great ideas for a port day.

-Mary Martin USA

Aptly titled, you won't just be a tourist after reading this book. You'll be greater than a tourist!

-Alan Warner, Grand Rapids, USA

Even though I only have three days to spend in San Miguel in an upcoming visit, I will use the author's suggestions to guide some of my time there. An easy read - with chapters named to guide me in directions I want to go.

-Robert Catapano, USA

Great insights from a local perspective! Useful information and a very good value!

-Sarah, USA

This series provides an in-depth experience through the eyes of a local. Reading these series will help you to travel the city in with confidence and it'll make your journey a unique one.

-Andrew Teoh, Ipoh, Malaysia

GREATER THAN A TOURIST – BRISBANE QUEENSLAND AUSTRALIA

50 Travel Tips from a Local

Claire Heath

https://pixabay.com/en/brisbane-queensland-australia-1251488/

Greater Than a Tourist
Visit our website at www.GreaterThanaTourist.com

Lock Haven, PA
All rights reserved.
ISBN: 9781983308550

>TOURIST

50 TRAVEL TIPS FROM A LOCAL

BOOK DESCRIPTION

Are you excited about planning your next trip?

Do you want to try something new?

Would you like some guidance from a local?

If you answered yes to any of these questions, then this Greater Than a Tourist book is for you.

Greater Than a Tourist – Brisbane, Queensland, Australia, by Claire Heath, offers the inside scoop on Queensland's capital city, which basks in a year-round great climate. Most travel books tell you how to travel like a tourist. Although there is nothing wrong with that, as part of the Greater Than a Tourist series, this book will give you travel tips from someone who has lived at your next travel destination.

In these pages, you will discover advice that will help you throughout your stay. This book will not tell you exact addresses or store hours but instead will give you excitement and knowledge from a local that you may not find in other smaller print travel books.

Travel like a local. Slow down, stay in one place, and get to know the people and the culture. By the time you finish this book, you will be eager and prepared to travel to your next destination.

TABLE OF CONTENTS

BOOK DESCRIPTION

TABLE OF CONTENTS

DEDICATION

ABOUT THE AUTHOR

HOW TO USE THIS BOOK

FROM THE PUBLISHER

OUR STORY

WELCOME TO

> TOURIST

INTRODUCTION

Before you arrive

1. Electric Australia

2. Travel lightly and consciously: water and plastic

3. Enjoy our glorious sunshine without roasting your skin

Arriving and getting around

4. G'day, mate!

5. Getting around Brisbane is easy on public transport

6. Driving in Brisbane (and Australia)

7. Even better, get on a bike

Places and stories about place

8. Introduce yourself to the original Queenslanders

9. See the Bangarra dancers perform

10. Brisbane City Hall is a step back in time

11. Historical houses and buildings illustrate the past
12. Go to university
13. Wander Wynnum
14. Northern bayside suburbs are a relaxing escape from the city centre
15. Sunnybank is where it's at for cheap, authentic Asian food

Short tours under your own steam

16. Ride along the river, ride on the river
17. Ride the river on the ferries
18. Ride a train or bus to the end of the line
19. Walk to King Island

Make the most of our parks

20. Mt Coot-tha is more than its summit lookout
21. Watch boats bob on the water from the city's green heart
22. Go to the beach
23. Picnic and play in the great suburban parks
24. Breathe in the fresh forest air of parks on the city's edge
25. Watch the sun set from Mount Gravatt

The islands

26. Take the ferry to North Stradbroke Island
27. Get the island vibe
28. Play (sensitively) on Moreton Island
29. Explore the islands in the bay

30. Get the feel of 'the hell-hole of the South Pacific'
31. Drive to Bribie Island
32. Go to the supermarket
33. And then go to the markets
34. Yes, there is a local fashion scene
35. Go on a treasure hunt
36. Get lost in the glorious (musty) world of pre-loved books
37. Go to the footy
38. Go to the cricket
39. Stretch and fold
40. Climb the walls
41. Swim at the oldest pool in the southern hemisphere

Culture, from highbrow to the street
42. Enjoy some art
43. Street art becomes mainstream
44. Go to the library
45. Go to the Ekka
46. Cinematheque

Entertainment
47. Get board
48. It's more than just a movie at Blue Room
49. Eating as entertainment
50. Specialty bars, from rooftops to below ground
Bonus 1. Chill out with some free live music

Bonus 2. All that jazz

Bonus 3. Enjoy the energy of Brisbane's flourishing
   live music scene

TOP REASONS TO BOOK THIS TRIP

50 THINGS TO KNOW ABOUT PACKING LIGHT
   FOR TRAVEL

Packing and Planning Tips

Travel Questions

Travel Bucket List

NOTES

DEDICATION

This book is dedicated to my family and the many friends I have made in Brisbane, all of whom continue to share its diversity with me.

ABOUT THE AUTHOR

I have lived in Brisbane for many years. I grew up on a farm and, like many rural children, when I became an adult, I gravitated to the city for university, work and the opportunities cities offer. Eventually, this led me to Brisbane. I remember vividly the moment I realised that I had put down roots here: this town was now my home.

I love to travel, and when I'm in an unfamiliar culture, I seek out the everyday activities and interests of the local people, because I'm curious about how others see the world and how they spend their time. To me, these are what make a place unique, and save it from the kind of homogenisation that seems to have spread with globalisation. I like to chat with shopkeepers and waiters, children selling tourist tat, old people sitting in the sun, and dogs hanging around. When I return home, I enjoy meeting looking at Brisbane afresh, with the same curiosity. It is a great antidote to taking the familiar for granted.

Some of my favourite things to do in Brisbane are listed in this book. I'm sure you'll discover your own.

I extend the warm Brisbane welcome to you. Maybe you'll enjoy your visit so much you will decide to stay for good!

HOW TO USE THIS BOOK

The Greater Than a Tourist book series was written by someone who has lived in an area for over three months. The goal of this book is to help travelers either dream or experience different locations by providing opinions from a local. The author has made suggestions based on their own experiences. Please do your own research before traveling to the area in case the suggested places are unavailable.

FROM THE PUBLISHER

Traveling can be one of the most important parts of a person's life. The anticipation and memories that you have are some of the best. As a publisher of the Greater Than a Tourist book series, as well as the popular 50 Things to Know book series, we strive to help you learn about new places, spark your imagination, and inspire you. Wherever you are and whatever you do I wish you safe, fun, and inspiring travel.

Lisa Rusczyk Ed. D.
CZYK Publishing

OUR STORY

Traveling is a passion of the "Greater than a Tourist" series creator. Lisa studied abroad in college, and for their honeymoon Lisa and her husband toured Europe. During her travels to Malta, an older man tried to give her some advice based on his own experience living on the island since he was a young boy. She was not sure if she should talk to the stranger but was interested in his advice. When traveling to some places she was wary to talk to locals because she was afraid that they weren't being genuine. Through her travels, Lisa learned how much locals had to share with tourists. Lisa created the "Greater Than a Tourist" book series to help connect people with locals. A topic that locals are very passionate about sharing.

WELCOME TO
> TOURIST

INTRODUCTION

"To awaken quite alone in a strange town is one of the most pleasant sensations in the world. You are surrounded by adventure."

— Freya Stark

Brisbane is the capital city of Australia's north-eastern state, Queensland. It used to have a reputation as daggy and dull. Not these days! Brisbane is a prosperous, modern city, with good infrastructure and an enormous range of activities that make the most of the balmy, subtropical climate. Strangely, though, it's still often overlooked by foreign visitors (and even other Australians). If they stay in Brisbane at all, it's usually only for a night or two as a stopover between Sydney or Melbourne and the Great Barrier Reef. But it's worth spending time in Brisbane, and getting to know the locals, and the city and its environs.

The climate is balmy, with wet summers and dry winters that are deliciously warm during the day, and cool at night. Even during the wetter months, there are plenty of dry days. (The official terminology is that we have a humid subtropical climate.) I like to think that the climate is one reason the people are laid-back and friendly. While it can be pretty hot and steamy from December to the end of February, and sometimes beyond, there are plenty of ways to keep cool, making Brisbane a great place to visit year-round.

In this guide, I won't tell you about the activities and places you can find repeated in tour guides (printed and online): Lone Pine, South Bank Parklands, Roma Street Parkland, climbing the Story Bridge, visiting Australia Zoo, tours of the XXXX (pronounced 'four-ex') Brewery, privately run cruises of the Brisbane River, feeding dolphins at Tangalooma, or taking in the view from the Mt Coot-tha lookout (although I do mention some of the other great things you can do in this park). There's already heaps of information about them online. I also don't give a lot of space to bars, cafes, restaurants, and pubs, or music venues, nightclubs and other party places. Not only do venues open and close regularly, so that it's almost impossible to remain accurate, you'll find them discussed and reviewed in many places online. (You probably already have.)

What I will share with you are some of the places locals love and frequent, the things we like to do around here—and the sort of insider information that I look for when I am travelling in foreign places. Many of the activities and places in this book are cheap, even free. Most of them are things I enjoy introducing out-of-town friends and family to.

The items listed here are a just a start: if you're happy to wander a street or two away from the well-trodden tourist streets, you're discover your very own Brisbane. Enjoy!

BEFORE YOU ARRIVE
1. ELECTRIC AUSTRALIA

Australia's mains electricity is 240 volts. If you are bringing appliances from Japan, Canada, or the USA, you may need a voltage converter as well as your power adapter.

Power sockets take Type I power plugs, which have three flat blades, the lower one vertical and the two upper ones at a 30° angle to the vertical. Most plugs have an earth to insulate you from shocks, although you will sometimes come across unearthed, two-pin plugs. These fit the standard Aussie three-hole power socket. (You can use the same power plugs in New Zealand.)

If you have sensitive or important piece of gear that needs access to power, you might want to invest in a surge protector to prevent a high-voltage spike frying its innards. It's only rarely that this happens, as the electricity infrastructure works well, but it can happen. For example, Brisbane has magnificent summer thunderstorms, which typically gather over a couple of days before finally letting loose. There can be some pretty powerful energy in these storms, and it's possible for a lightning strike to wipe out gear connected to the power. You can buy surge protectors cheaply here. A cheaper option is to unplug your gear when a storm rolls over.

2. TRAVEL LIGHTLY AND CONSCIOUSLY: WATER AND PLASTIC

Australia is the second driest continent, and even though Brisbane is in the subtropics, it can get pretty dry here, too. (The dry season is, roughly, from April to October; most of our rain falls between November and the March, although it varies year to year and climate change seems to be making it more variable.) The climate of much of the country, including south-east Queensland, is characterised by dry periods and even droughts, which are in some years relieved by wetter seasons. This means that, even in a good year, water isn't as abundant as it is in most other parts of the world. Help us conserve water by taking short showers (of no more than four minutes), turning the tap off while you are brushing your teeth, and, when washing up, putting the plug in the sink and running a little water into it, rather than washing under a running tap (a common practice in many parts of the world).

Brisbane tap water is potable (drinkable), so you don't need to buy bottled water. So … please don't. As you know, the plastic waste from the consumption of bottled water is a growing problem world-wide, not just in Australia, even though here we might not see how big the problem is because rubbish collection is efficient. Take a bottle with you as you explore. Most cafes will refill it from the tap for you, and you can also refill it from the water bubblers dotted around the city in parks and along popular pedestrian streets.

Please ask staff at cafes and bars not to put a straw in your drink.

On the subject of plastic, please encourage us (and our supermarkets and shops) to learn how to shop without single-use plastic bags. You can do this by refusing to buy pre-packaged fresh produce, and refusing grocery bags at the check-out—Australia is a bit behind the times in this regard. Take a reusable shopping bag with you. One option is Australia's very own Onya bag. ('Onya' is short you 'on you', as in 'Good onya, mate, well done!') The original bag was about the size of a supermarket grocery bag; these days there is a whole product line. The original folds into itself and will then fit in the palm of your hand. It's also very light. I have had the same bag for 15

19

years, and take it with me wherever I travel in the world; it may be the best-travelled bag in the world! Onya (and other companies) also have re-usable produce bags and lightweight back-packs, among other useful things. Please re-use whatever plastic bags you do end up with, and take them to hold fruit and vegetables you buy at the market or greengrocers.

3. ENJOY OUR GLORIOUS SUNSHINE WITHOUT ROASTING YOUR SKIN

Queenslanders pride ourselves on our sunny weather. But beware: we also have the dubious record of being the skin-cancer capital of the world. Which means that the sun here is strong. Here comes my spoilsport advice: the Cancer Council of Queensland recommends that, whenever you are outside, you wear a hat with a broad brim, a shirt (one with long sleeves and a collar is best), and sunglasses, and use water-resistant sunscreen with a sun-protection factor (SPF) of 30. Hang out in the shade when you can, especially between 10 am and 4 pm. (I know, I know; you've come here to soak up the sun.) Keep in mind that you can get badly burned even in winter.

Because of the incidence of skin cancer, there are some really good Australian-manufactured sunscreens around. They are available in chemists everywhere, so you don't need to bring any with you. Bonus: if you buy your sunscreen at a Cancer Council shop, you will be contributing to cancer research.

Do some research before buying sunscreen: get a brand that doesn't contain microbeads. If you are going to the Great Barrier Reef or other fragile watery environments, research the environmental safety of the brand you want to buy: sunscreen washing off bodies in the water is beginning to pollute parts of the reef, and may contribute to disease in corals and other reef life. (One reason for this is that spending energy fighting off pollutants makes them weaker, which makes them less able to stave off the effects of coral bleaching, sediment in the water, and other nasties.)

ARRIVING AND GETTING AROUND
4. G'DAY, MATE!

G'day, mate, and welcome to Brisbane. Yeah, the greeting sounds corny and very mid-20th century, but you will often hear locals say 'G'day' to you. I've even been welcomed home this way by customs officers at the international airport.

If you are driving or cycling into Brisbane, you'll probably have a smartphone map to guide you to your 'home' here. If you are arriving by plane, bus, or train, various local transport options will get you to your accommodation. The Airtrain connects the domestic and international airport terminals into the city and suburban train and bus network, and can take you directly to Redcliffe (on the northern edge of Brisbane and Moreton Bay), and to the Gold Coast and the theme parks at Coomera.

You can also leave the airport using a taxi, an Uber, or a city-bound shuttle bus.

The long-distance trains end their journey at the transit centre on Roma Street, on the edge of the city's central business district (CBD). This is also where the interstate and regional buses arrive (and leave from). All Brisbane suburban trains go through Roma Street, and several city buses stop outside the centre, so you can easily connect into the urban public transport network.

When I'm going to the airport, I like to take the Airtrain, as it sticks to its schedule (published online), so I can guarantee my arrival time. You can't do this in private cars or taxis, because the amount of traffic congestion fluctuates. If there's an accident on the network of freeways, or other road congestion, traffic may back up, delaying your arrival by up to 45 minutes, and sometimes an hour.

5. GETTING AROUND BRISBANE IS EASY ON PUBLIC TRANSPORT

If you don't have your own car, a great way to get around Brisbane is on the network of buses, trains and ferries, which are all air-conditioned. The network is run by TransLink. You can buy individual tickets for most services as you get on, but it's much cheaper to use TransLink's Gocard. Buy a card from some train stations, or from many newsagents and 7–Eleven stores, put credit on it, and you're ready to explore. (You can top up the credit on your card at these places, too. Newsagents that sell cards and top-ups usually have a Gocard poster displayed at the shop entrance.) To use the card, touch it against a card reader at the beginning and end of each stage of your trip. You'll see the readers at each train station, and on all buses and ferries. If your trip involves two or more changes, the card will charge you for one journey.

The TransLink website has more details about how to use the card. It also tells you how to get back any credit remaining on the card when you leave Brisbane (if you don't stay and become a local, that is). The website has some information in languages other than English, too.

For some services, such as the City Flyer express bus, you can only use a Gocard; drivers don't sell individual tickets. Again, the TransLink website will give you details.

The website also has a useful journey planner, to help you work out which service you need.

6. DRIVING IN BRISBANE (AND AUSTRALIA)

If you want to flexibility of a car and don't come with your own, check out the Car Next Door online. It's like Airbnb for transport.

In Australia, we drive on the left-hand side of the road. Most cars these days have an automatic transmission, which makes the switch to driving on our side of the road easier to get used to. Responsibility for drivers' licences, and the rules under which they are granted, lie with each state government (not the national government). In Queensland, the Department of Transport and Main Roads is the responsible authority. Of course, to drive you'll need a valid driver's licence. Details are available from the Queensland Government website.

When you are out walking, please (please, please) remember to mindfully check—in both directions—before crossing roads. There are much better ways to enjoy Brisbane than from a hospital bed.

Brisbanites can be pretty relaxed—but not when it comes to paying for metered or private parking. The authorities are not lenient with visitors, and if you don't pay for a metered space, or overstay the time you've paid for or the free-parking limit, don't be surprised if you find a ticket under a windscreen wiper. I suspect the parking inspectors are trained in charm deflection, as I've not seen anyone charm themselves out of a ticket in recent years.

There are six toll roads in Brisbane. As there are no toll gates; tolls are calculated electronically as you pass a tolling point. You pay online, either by setting up an account (useful if you're driving a lot) or to pay for an occasional journey. For the latter, you must pay within three days of using the toll road. If you've rented a vehicle, ask the rental company about paying for tolls. Or research your options online. (Try entering the search term 'Queensland toll road' or 'Linkt'.) You will probably be able to find a free alternative route if you don't want to pay tolls. (Toll roads are a controversial subject in Brisbane, something it might be fun to discuss with new-found local friends over a beer.)

7. EVEN BETTER, GET ON A BIKE

Even better than using private vehicles (or even public transport) is cycling around the city. If you have your own bike, great. If not, the Brisbane City Council's CityCycle scheme is available for residents and visitors alike. It operates in the same way as other public bicycle schemes around the world: you pay and collect a bike from one of the dozens of stations around the city, and drop it off at any of them.

You can become a member or buy a casual pass. The first half hour of your ride is free, so if you aren't going far, you may not pay anything for your ride.

The CityCyle website has all the details. There's also an app that helps you locate stations nearby. If you have a Gocard, you can use this to pay for bike hire.

One thing to remember: under Australian law, you have to wear a helmet when cycling anywhere in the country. The police do fine people for not wearing them. Some CityCycle bikes come with helmets. Most locals I know who use the scheme carry a hair net or cap with them, to use as a liner inside the helmet.

PLACES AND STORIES ABOUT PLACE

8. INTRODUCE YOURSELF TO THE ORIGINAL QUEENSLANDERS

On the ground floor of the State Library of Queensland (SLQ) you'll find kuril dhagun, a space that celebrates Queensland's Aboriginal and Torres Strait Islands cultures. The name means 'place of the water rat' in one of the local Aboriginal languages: kuril is the native water rat, which can still be found in this reach of the Brisbane River, and dhagun translates as 'place' or 'country'. This is a great place to learn more about the first Australians. Check the SLQ's website for activities and events at kuril dhagun, or drop in and find out about contemporary issues from the current exhibition and from local Indigenous news media kept here.

9. SEE THE BANGARRA DANCERS PERFORM

You can gain a better appreciation of one facet of contemporary Indigenous Australia by catching a performance by Bangarra Dance Theatre. This is an Aboriginal and Torres Strait Islander company, and one of the most exciting performance groups in Brisbane. Bangarra stages theatrical, powerful dance, mostly telling Indigenous stories from an Indigenous point of view. The company also works with Aboriginal and Torres Strait children and young people to nurture their pride in their cultures, and teach dance to the next generation.

10. BRISBANE CITY HALL IS A STEP BACK IN TIME

Brisbane doesn't have many beautiful old buildings, but there are a few to be found. The city hall is one of them. It was built in the 1920s, and is full of the architectural grace of the time. The Museum of Brisbane, which is housed in the building, runs several free tours of the hall, its clock tower, and nearby Roma Street Parkland. The museum often has interesting exhibitions, too, mostly concerning some aspect of the history of the city, including current events.

11. HISTORICAL HOUSES AND BUILDINGS ILLUSTRATE THE PAST

If historical houses are your thing, you'll see a classy example of Victorian age iron-lace and building style in a visit to Miegunyah House, in the inner-city suburb of Bowen Hills. The house is open for tours—and morning and afternoon teas. It's run by the Queensland Women's Historical Association, whose members give monthly talks in the formal dining room.

You might also like to check out Newstead House, which is set in spacious grounds that slope down to the Brisbane River (read: picnic). Another historic house open to visitors is Wolston House, the oldest surviving farmhouse in Brisbane.

Famous tin-and-timber architecture is still lovingly maintained by homeowners and small business people in many inner suburbs. Wander the streets of Spring Hill, Paddington, and other suburbs near the city. The Regatta Hotel has been gracing the river at Toowong. It's been quenching the thirst of Brisbanites, including, in recent decades, the very thirsty students of the University of Queensland, for 140 years. The hotel is also the setting for a famous moment in local feminist history: in 1965, Merle Thornton and Rosalie Bogner chained themselves to the public bar when the barkeep refused to serve them because they were female. In fairness, he couldn't without breaking the law, which is what the women were protesting about. Their actions led to pub doors being opened to women, too.

12. GO TO UNIVERSITY

Two of Brisbane's three universities—Griffith University and the University of Queensland (UQ)—have lovely grounds that you can enjoy free. And the third one, Queensland University of Technology (QUT), has a city campus that sits next to the city botanical gardens. They are all attractive places to wile away a few hours, or to picnic in.

UQ lies in a bend of the Brisbane River opposite West End. To get there, ride a CityCyle, or take a CityCat ferry or a bus. The grounds are landscaped and in places feel a little like an old English estate, with lawns dotted with mature shade trees. Stroll along the path that hugs the river, or take one of the paths that go by the lake, which is close to the ferry stop and the bus station near the 'green' bridge. Shady trees and gentle slopes are ideal for a picnic, and you can enjoy the antics of the resident ducks, too. It's especially lovely in October, when the numerous jacaranda trees are flowering.

Griffith University has two campuses close together, in the suburbs of Nathan and Mount Gravatt. They are connected by Toohey Forest, which is a stretch of beautiful and relatively undisturbed eucalypt bushland that is native to the area. Paths for walking and cycling connect the forest and the two campuses. Take a picnic lunch with you, and chill out with the bush birds. If you stop and stand quietly for a while, you may be lucky enough to spot one of the koalas that is native to the area. They can be very hard to see, so you may be able to spot the trees they're in by searching for scats (poo) at the base of trees. The forest is also home to many species of birds, reptiles, frogs and butterflies. If you are in Brisbane in late winter or the first half of spring (August–September) you'll also see lots of plants in bloom. Brisbane City Council's website has information on Toohey Forest and bike and foot paths that link it to Griffith University. Public transport access is by bus, or you can take CityCycle and use the network of bike paths to get there.

At QUT, you can combine great coffee on campus and a visit to the elegant colonial sandstone building Old Government House, in the heart of the campus, with a stroll through the gardens.

13. WANDER WYNNUM

Wynnum, Manly and Lota are low-key bayside suburbs that feel more relaxed than the suburbs near the city centre. It's great to walk or cycle along the waterfront: no matter what the weather, the bay is always beautiful in its ever-changing moods. Farmers' markets (for produce) and craft markets at are held regularly at Manly's Little Bayside Park. There are plenty of waterside places for kids to play at. And there is a growing food scene in this part of the bay, including several cafes on the water at Manly Boat Harbour. At the northern end of Wynnum, there's a quiet nook of mangroves reached by a boardwalk over the water. You can look through the leaves of the trees across the bay, which on weekends will be dotted with the sails of locals out racing.

14. NORTHERN BAYSIDE SUBURBS ARE A RELAXING ESCAPE FROM THE CITY CENTRE

The northern bayside suburbs of Brighton, Redcliffe, Sandgate, Scarborough, and Shorncliffe were once separate villages. In the early 20th century, many of them became popular places for urban Brisbanites to escape the stresses of the city. Even though they are part of the greater Brisbane area now, they are still places we love to escape to! They've retained something of the atmosphere of a coastal village, and feel a world away from the urban vibe of the city's centre. They are less than an hour from the CBD on the train. Picnic on the beach at Sandgate: get there early, as locals love to hang out for leisurely picnics on a weekend, and the tables are usually taken by mid-morning. Or stroll the length of the Shorncliffe pier. There's a lovely old pier to walk out on, too, and the water is calm and enjoyable for swimming.

Another activity that's popular with us locals is to walk or cycle from Shorncliffe to Scarborough and back, enjoying fish and chips at either end—or both.

In fact, the whole coastline has networks of waterfront paths that are wonderful to walk along.

15. SUNNYBANK IS WHERE IT'S AT FOR CHEAP, AUTHENTIC ASIAN FOOD

Forget Chinatown; these days, Sunnybank is Brisbane's 'Little Asia'. Head to the shopping centres that cluster around the intersection of the very busy thoroughfares of Mains Road and McCullough Street and search out cheap, authentic cafes and restaurants, as well as produce-sellers that are packed doing business with Brisbanites who hail from south-east Asia. The drab shopping mall of Sunnybank Plaza harbours many south-east Asian eateries. In Market Square, diagonally across the intersection, the smells alone will take you to south-east Asia. Don't be surprised if the menu is written without a word of English.

SHORT TOURS UNDER YOUR OWN STEAM

16. RIDE ALONG THE RIVER, RIDE ON THE RIVER

A wonderful bikeway hugs the city and inner-suburban reaches of the Brisbane River, and it's well worth making like a local and spinning your pedals along it. Along the way, you'll come across plenty of cafes and picnic areas to catch your breath or enjoy a spot of people watching. A part of the bikeway that lies over the river itself was washed away in a flood in 2011, but this much-loved corridor has been rebuilt and is as popular as ever. From New Farm Park and the Powerhouse, where you might take in an exhibition or sample the tasty tucker (food), you can ride along the waterfront nearly the whole way to the city botanical gardens. After passing through the gardens, you can stay on the city side of the river and take the bikeway under the freeway and through a few quiet suburban streets all the way to the University of Queensland and beyond. Or you can cross the river at the Goodwill or Kurilpa pedestrian bridges, and continue riding. If you turn south, you can make a circuit by cycling under the Kangaroo Point cliffs to the end of the point under the Story

Bridge, and then ride over the bridge and join the bikeway on the other side, or head into Fortitude Valley. If you turn north, you can take bikeway and quiet streets to Orleigh Park in West End.

You can do all these on foot, too.

17. RIDE THE RIVER ON THE FERRIES

Seeing the city from the vantage point of the river is a favourite with locals.

The CityCat catamaran ferries ply the Brisbane River from Hamilton, in the north-east, passing the city centre and South Bank Parklands, to the University of Queensland south of the city centre. It's fun to go the length of the route, and see the city from the river gives you a new perspective on it.

Another way to travel the river—and this option is free—is on the cute wooden CityHopper ferries. These cute, wooden ferries hark back to the inner-city service that was replaced by the expanded CityCat service. The old ferries were repainted in red and white, and putter up and down the river between North Quay in the city centre and Sydney Street, in New Farm, stopping at eight terminals on both sides of the river. The CityHopper runs every half hour from 6 am to midnight. Why not disembark at Eagle Street Pier, and stop at Jade Buddha, at Riverside, for a drink. Or get off in New Farm, to see an exhibition or show at the Powerhouse.

The city council also runs two paid cross-river ferries between the city centre (Eagle Street Pier), and Kangaroo Point (Holman Street and Thornton Street). These run every 10–15 minutes.

18. RIDE A TRAIN OR BUS TO THE END OF THE LINE

Something I like to do in new places is jump on a train or a bus, and take it to the end of the line. It's a great way to see suburban life in action, and to see the unique character of different parts of the city. In Brisbane, you can use the city train network to get to the Gold Coast (in the south), the Sunshine Coast (in the north), and Ipswich (in the south-west). At the coastal terminals, the trains connect to local buses that can take you to some of the country's best white-sand beaches. And Ipswich has a wonderful store of colonial and federation wooden architecture, as well as numerous antique and retro shops to explore, markets, and a growing list of cafes.

19. WALK TO KING ISLAND

South of Wynnum and Manly is Wellington Point. It's fun to be there at low tide, to walk to King Island along the 1 km-long sandbar that is exposed at low tide. Be sure to check when the tide is out, though! Wellington Point has some great cafes, too, as well as green areas for picnics if you want to cater for yourself.

MAKE THE MOST OF OUR PARKS

20. MT COOT-THA IS MORE THAN ITS SUMMIT LOOKOUT

Mt Coot-tha offers much more than its famous summit view, impressive though that is. (On a clear day, you can see the islands of Moreton Bay.) JC Slaughter Falls is popular for picnics, and from here you can walk to the summit on one of the most popular trails in the park. There are numerous other tracks, though, that are well worth taking. There are maps of the trails dotted around the park, and you can easily join several into a longer walk. Most are through open eucalypt forest. One of my favourites is the steep Powerful Owl Track, which is guaranteed to get your heart pumping. Mt Coot-tha is also where

39

you'll find the planetarium, and the second and larger of the city's botanical gardens. These gardens were established in the early 1970s, and have some wonderful large trees. The gardens cover a large area, and the collections are grouped by climate type. I admire the cactus collection (even though I'm not a cactus fancier), and the herbarium, next door, which has changing exhibitions with a botanical theme.

21. WATCH BOATS BOB ON THE WATER FROM THE CITY'S GREEN HEART

The city botanical gardens strike a different note, with a subtropical rainforest feel about it, albeit a manicured one. City workers and students dot the park during lunchtimes. There is a boardwalk through the mangroves on the river bank, and the shady trees further along make a nice place to sit and watch the boats bobbing at their moorings, with Kangaroo Point cliffs behind them. The riverside path is popular with cyclists, too, as it is part of the city bikeway.

22. GO TO THE BEACH

Think 'beach'—and you don't think of Brisbane. But lying peacefully just north of the Brisbane airport is Nudgee Beach, lapped by the gentle waters of Moreton Bay. This sheltered nook barely seems to be in the middle of a city. It's a lovely spot for a picnic, to sit and read a book, and to watch birds. (The beach is a protected habitat for birds.) It's also fantastic for sunrise reflections. And it's rarely, if ever, crowded.

23. PICNIC AND PLAY IN THE GREAT SUBURBAN PARKS

By now you will have gathered that Brisbane has some fantastic parks. Most have shady trees and open areas of clipped lawns; and many provide children's play areas and free barbecues (put in and maintained by the city council). They're great for picnics, a game of Frisbee or impromptu football, a stroll, reading, and watching the locals at play. Among the most popular with locals are New Farm Park, which has a fabulous children's play area that includes a great fort-like climbing structure and a 'spider web' climbing net under the shade of enormous figs that are more than 100 years old. It is next to the Powerhouse. Orleigh Park in West End, and the parks at the top and the base of Kangaroo Point cliffs are other great favourites in the inner city. You can hire kayaks at Kangaroo Point Cliffs, and paddle along the

41

river. All these parks are easily to access by bicycle or public transport.

A little further afield, Sherwood Arboretum is great for adults and kids, big and small, and has playgrounds, picnic spots, and magnificent eucalypts in a park setting along a stretch of the Brisbane River. It's an easy walk from Sherwood train station.

The Rocks Riverside Park at Seventeen Mile Rocks has extensive lawns for picnics and play. The park lies on river flats of the Brisbane River, and features public art that reflects the previous industrial history of the area. Among the cool play equipment in the park is a climbing net and a flying fox (zipline)— but they are strictly for children.

On the southside is Daisy Hill Conservation Park. It's an area of sun-dappled eucalypt forest and paperbark wetlands, with plentiful trails for walking, mountain biking, and horse-riding. It's also a great picnic spot. Koalas are native to this part of Brisbane, and the Queensland Government runs a koala centre at Daisy Hill. Most of the koalas at the centre have been brought in to be treated for illnesses. You can wander through the large enclosure and look for them dozing safely in the trees. You can't hold these koalas, but it is a treat to see them in a more-or-less natural setting. Wildlife officers give daily talks about koalas, so check the web for current times. Entrance to the centre is free.

24. BREATHE IN THE FRESH FOREST AIR OF PARKS ON THE CITY'S EDGE

Some bushland parks around the edge of Brisbane offer graded walking tracks through native bushland, as well as picnic areas. Each park has its own character, and is well worth a half day or day of walking. Anyone with moderate fitness will manage the walking tracks in these parks.

Bounding the city in the north-west is D'Aguilar National Park (which you may hear locals call Brisbane Forest Park). It has numerous trails through remnants of the original forests of the area: eucalypt woodland and dry rainforest. So does nearby Mt Glorious. A favourite short walk here is the Thylogale Track, which leaves from Jollys Lookout. (Thylogale is the scientific group name for the pademelons, small marsupials in the same family as kangaroos.) You'll need access to a car for this park.

Bullocky Rest, on Lake Samsonvale, is a favourite picnic area of northside families. There are children's playgrounds, and you can fish in the lake—it can only be using line, and you need a permit, which is sold by the Queensland Government. (It's not expensive.)

The name of the picnic area rings with Queensland's colonial history. A bullocky is someone who drives the bullock teams that were used to pull drays loaded with freight (such as provisions for rural families, and timber) between farmsteads and settlements. In those days, Brisbane was not much more than a village on the banks of the sleepy river, and this area was remote bush.

25. WATCH THE SUN SET FROM MOUNT GRAVATT

The summit of Mount Gravatt is a great place to watch the sun set over Brisbane and the mountains behind it. It's quieter than Mt Coot-tha, so if you prefer peaceful, this spot may be better for you. There are some walking trails here, too, so come earlier to combine a hike with the sunset. It's a popular activity among locals, so if you're driving get there early to get a parking space. The road to the summit is very popular with cyclists, who use it for hills training, so be on the lookout for them.

THE ISLANDS

26. TAKE THE FERRY TO NORTH STRADBROKE ISLAND

Moreton Bay is protected from the open ocean by North Stradbroke Island and Moreton Island. Both islands are made of sand. Numerous smaller islands dot the bay, and some of these are easy to visit using public transport.

North Stradbroke, or Straddie as we call it, is easy to get to using public transport. Take a train to Cleveland, where you will be met by a free shuttle bus. It connects you to the two ferry companies that run vehicular and passenger ferries to Dunwich, on the protected mainland side of the island. (The passenger ferry is known as the water taxi.) Most ferry services link with the island bus service, which goes to Amity Point and Point Lookout.

Among the favourite local activities, it is hard to beat sipping a beer or eating lunch at the Point Lookout pub as you look over the ocean. On the point itself, buy fish and chips and head across the road to the steeply sloping grass of the headland to take in the blue of the ocean and sky as you munch local fish (and lick your fingers afterwards). There is a small

45

gorge at the point, and a walking track and boardwalk takes you around the headland through wallum bushland, plants that have managed to be beautiful and thrive in sand and salty air. You'll often see wallabies (the smaller, prettier cousins of kangaroos), and you'll have fantastic views over the ocean. From the lookouts, you can see turtles gliding through the waves dashing against the rocks, or pods of dolphins surfing the waves. Further our, between June and October, humpback whales frolic, slapping the surface with their flukes or spouting water. It's the best place for free whale watching!

When you return to the mainland, I recommend getting to Dunwich well ahead of the ferry's departure time, so you have time to stop at the Little Ship Club for a beer. It has grassy lawns right to the water's edge, and it's a great spot for sipping a coldie and watching the sun set over the bay and the mainland.

27. GET THE ISLAND VIBE

I said I wouldn't spare space for music, but I can't resist recommending one of my favourite music festivals, our home-grown Island Vibe. It's held on North Stradbroke Island every October. It's a great time of year to be on the island (the sun isn't too fierce yet), and the festival has a relaxed and friendly atmosphere. Another plus is that it celebrates the culture of the local Aboriginal people, the Quandamooka, and the festival line-up includes Indigenous bands. (The Quandamooka name for the island is Minjerribah.) If you want to go to the festival, book your accommodation, even if it's a tent site, well ahead of the event, as accommodation gets booked out. If Point Lookout is full, you can camp at Amity Point, which is pretty and quiet. The festival organisers run a shuttle bus between Amity and the festival site.

While you're on the island, stop at the Salt Water Murris Quandamooka art gallery, at Dunwich (where the ferry from the mainland docks), and talk to some of the locals about their ways and world view.

28. PLAY (SENSITIVELY) ON MORETON ISLAND

You can also see humpback whales from Moreton Island. This island isn't quite as easy to get to as Straddie, as its further from the mainland, but vehicle barges (which take walk-on passengers, too) and ferries go to and from the island every day. (A web search will give you the current information on services, timetables, and prices.) The island isn't as developed as Straddie, which is part of its charm, so unless you have your own 4WD vehicle, if you want to go further afield than Tangalooma resort, you'll be up for a paid tour. One of my favourite things to do is to snorkel around the Tangalooma wrecks. The boats that make this small 'reef' were sunk deliberately to create a safe place for small boats to anchor, as the wrecks protect them from the swell. This artificial environment has become the home of corals and tropical fish—and you can let your imagination go wild imagining new stories for the rusting hulks.

I've camped many a time at the Blue Lagoon campsite, near the northern point of the island. If you go to Blue Lagoon, please consider your impact on this fragile environment. One thing you can do is enjoy the lagoon by swimming in its lovely waters and not taking part in mud-bathing tours. This has become a really popular activity—but it is damaging the natural life of the lagoon, as the mud on the bottom is continually stirred up, which is not something the local wildlife have evolved to cope with. A walk along the sea shore to the lighthouse at Cape Moreton will fill your lungs with fresh, salty air.

Be careful if you go swimming on the ocean side of the island, as there are often invisible rips and currents, even when the water looks calm.

29. EXPLORE THE ISLANDS IN THE BAY

Several smaller islands in the bay are fun to visit, too. Coochiemudlo Island is a pretty little residential island a few kilometres from Victoria Point, in the southern bay. It takes about 10 minutes on the ferry to get there. It's small enough that you can circumnavigate it in about an hour. You can also wile away time watching wildlife, fishing, swimming … or you could laze about: be flat out like a lizard drinking, as we say. There's a rich variety of birdlife, including the regal white-bellied sea eagle. In the water, it's possible to spot turtles, dugongs, and dolphins. The island is a great, safe play space for children.

A ferry service connects the mainland to the southern islands of Karragarra, Lamb, Russell, and MacLeay. You can jump on and jump off as you please. The TransLink website has the schedule. MacLeay Island has some lovely swimming coves, and there is accommodation and cafes should you decide you can't bear to leave the relaxed atmosphere and return to Brisbane.

30. GET THE FEEL OF 'THE HELL-HOLE OF THE SOUTH PACIFIC'

Another small island in Moreton Bay is St Helena. The island functioned as a prison for 65 years. Although it was known as 'the hell-hole of the South Pacific' it was, apparently, one of the better (read: least brutal) prisons of the time. Although it is only a few kilometres from the mouth of the Brisbane River, that was distance enough to prevent prisoners getting back to Brisbane. Today, only a few ruins of buildings and other infrastructure remain, but the history tour of the island is told in an engaging way that makes the trip worthwhile. You can only visit the island on a paid tour.

If you want to avoid scores of schoolchildren, organise your tour for a weekend.

31. DRIVE TO BRIBIE ISLAND

Bribie Island makes the northern edge of Moreton Bay, and is the only bay island accessible by road, which is from the highway to the Sunshine Coast. Go by car, or check the TransLink website for details on how to get there by public transport. Sleepy Bribie Passage, which separates the island from the mainland, is a great place to go kayaking, fishing (from a boat or kayak) or stand-up paddle boarding. Vessels are available for hire at Bongaree. A walk along Sylvan Beach Esplanade gives you views of the passage through the line of paperbark trees (a type of eucalyptus). Afterwards, head to the ocean side to Woorim, where you can surf at the beach, which is patrolled by life savers. Hungry now? The pub and several cafes can help solve that problem! The pub is usually packed on weekends.

Shopping and window shopping

32. GO TO THE SUPERMARKET

Go to the supermarket Yes, really! I dislike grocery shopping at home (oh, how I dislike it!), but in a new culture I find it fascinating: I learn so many little details about how locals live by seeing what groceries are stocked. You can't learn this about a culture from visiting its churches and museums!

33. AND THEN GO TO THE MARKETS

Groceries are generally cheaper at the supermarket, but you'll often find cheaper fruit, vegetables and fresh meats at the markets. Organic produce is much cheaper at the suburban produce markets than in supermarkets and greengrocers. Most markets are held on weekends. However, if you find yourself in the city on a Wednesday around lunchtime, head to Reddacliff Place, across the street from the southern end of Queen Street, and join the throngs of city workers eating street food-style meals, and buying fresh and cottage-industry produce. It's pricey, but there is some delicious food on offer.

Goods at the weekend markets vary from upmarket to prices lower than the supermarket. Some of them sell art, clothing, jewellery, and homewares as well as groceries and food. Popular fresh produce markets are at Rocklea (which also has a good selection of cut flowers; on Saturdays), New Farm, West End, Wynnum, Milton, and Eagle Farm. Most of the markets are open in the mornings, but check websites for precise times. There are several popular weekend markets for bric-a-brac and craft or cottage-industry homewares, clothing, cosmetics and the like. Check out those at South Bank, which also has a regular young designers market, Riverside (in the city), and Rocklea (Sundays). Also worth exploring is the handmade expo held at Ipswich.

The West End market is set under spreading fig trees that are well over 100 years old. They provide welcome shade in summer. It's great to sit on the bank under one of these trees and chat to friends while listening to live music over a coffee and snack. This market is enormously popular with Brisbanites (read: it gets crowded—which is part of the fun).

At Northey Street, just north of the city (and an easy bus or bike ride away) is a weekly organic market. It's right next to a permaculture garden, the Northey Street City Farm, which is fun to wander around. The other fresh-produce markets also have stalls that sell organic produce, but Northey Street has a policy to sell organics only.

34. YES, THERE IS A LOCAL FASHION SCENE

Melbourne is recognised as the country's style capital, but there is some pretty cool—subtropical—style happening in Brisbane, too. If you like shopping, and you're into unique, local designs, hot-foot it to the James Street precinct in Teneriffe. Here you will find up-market local designers, as well as young designers experimenting with new, exciting ideas. You'll find clothing shops scattered along the streets that head towards the city and Fortitude Valley—particularly Ann, Wickham, and Brunswick streets, and the laneways that run off them. Brisbane designers with shopfronts include Dogstar, Maiocchi and Tengdahl for women's clothing, and The Cloakroom and Apartment for men's.

There are some gorgeous things to gaze at, even if you have no intention of buying. For more casual, and cheaper, options, check out the light-hearted designs of Jerico Road Clothing, The Happy Cabin, and Alice Nightingale. (I love Alice's budgie smuggler purse, a reference to a piece of Aussie slang that enjoyed a resurgence in popularity driven by the swimwear-clad photo opportunities sought out by a recent prime minister.) Check online for these and other up and coming designers; outlets and labels come and go regularly.

There are some great shops for clothes, footwear and accessories in Clayfield and the upmarket suburb of Ascot, too. In the inner-western suburb of Paddington, you'll find more quirky or upmarket designers. It's a great area to wander around, with junk shops, vintage and retro shops, bars, cafes, and small craft shops, all set out in the atmospheric tin-and-timber architecture that is quintessentially Queensland.

Vintage style is to be found also in the shopping streets of the suburbs of West End, Annerley, Rosalie, and Fortitude Valley. Many suburbs have op shops (opportunity shops, which sell second-hand clothing and household items that have been donated). These shops are run by charities such as St Vincent de Paul (which we nickname Vinnies), the Salvation Army (or the Salvos) and Lifeline to fund their programs. They are the cheapest places to shop for clothing, and they're found in most suburbs. You'll have to hunt through the racks, but you're likely to be rewarded with something you love.

35. GO ON A TREASURE HUNT

The pedestrian-friendly last (or is it first?) two blocks of Logan Road, in Woolloongabba, have long been home to a row of antique and second-hand stores. They are fast disappearing as Woolloongabba becomes gentrified, but there are still a few there. They are fun to spend time in, and you could well find some small treasures to take with you. In this stretch of street there's also a wonderful, atmospheric shop where violins are made by hand. It's often closed, but the window display is worth stopping for. The upside of gentrification is that there are plenty of tasty eating and drinking options in the area.

If you head from here along Ipswich Road to Annerley, you'll find a string of thrift stores selling antiques, retro stuff, second-hand books, scrapbooking supplies—and there's good coffee to be had.

Paddington has similar shops, but it's a more expensive area and that is reflected in the items on offer and their price tags. If you're in that area, extend your visit and head to nearby Newmarket to Shabby Treasures Down the Lane.

At Rocklea, you'll find Three Red Bikes, and in suburban Oxley, Revolve, Inc. There are more antique, vintage and treasure shops in the nearby suburbs.

36. GET LOST IN THE GLORIOUS (MUSTY) WORLD OF PRE-LOVED BOOKS

You can do much better for second-hand books than the local hostel bookshelf. Brisbane has some great second-hand bookshops. Bent in West End is a local institution, and has a much larger collection than its shopfront suggests. In the city, Archives Fine Books is an Aladdin's cave of second-hand and rare books. Well, it's actually in a brick warehouse that was built in the early 20th century, but you just might find a lamp with a genie inside as well as a good book. This bookshop has been in this spot since well before I arrived in Brisbane. The Clarence Corner Book Shop, near the Mater Hospital, has some great books, and reading tables to sit at. It's fun to browse the books over a coffee. (And the pub across the road has a microbrewery.) If you want to help others, head to the Annerley Community Bookshop. It's staffed by volunteers, and sales help fund literacy programs for refugees.

Sport

37. GO TO THE FOOTY

Australians have a reputation for playing sport, and even if that's still true, we love to watch it as well. Why not join us at some of our favourite spectator sports? If you're around any time from mid-March to the end of September, get yourself to a footy game for a slice of popular sport.

There are three football codes played in Australia: rugby league, rugby union, and the home-grown variety, Aussie rules (also known as AFL, for the Australian Football League that runs the national competition). (The round-ball game is known as soccer here.) The home ground of the Brisbane Lions AFL team is the Gabba, and on at-home game days, the streets around it are awash with people in the team's maroon and gold colours. Aussie rules began in Victoria in the 1800s. It's believed to have developed from a ball game played by the local Aboriginal people. Victoria remains the stronghold of Aussie rules, and Victoria fields the greatest number of the 18 teams in the national competition. A national women's competition began in 2017 between eight teams.

38. GO TO THE CRICKET

Long before the rest of the world had heard of Aussie rules, the Gabba became a sporting institution as a venue for state, national and international cricket. It's a summer sport, and the first international games start around November, as the days heat up and lengthen.

The Gabba traditionally hosts the first international Test match of the Aussie summer. The soundtrack of my childhood summer holidays was the cricket on TV, with the sound turned down so Dad could listen to the better commentary on the radio, so my favourite game is still the five-day Test match. But there is something about the energy and pace of the limited-over or single-day games that is hard to beat. Go with a local who can explain the rules.

39. STRETCH AND FOLD

After sitting watching others run around like mad things, you might loosen up those cramped muscles with a yoga session or more. There are plenty of styles, and many more venues, all over Brisbane. Many places offer specials for first-time visitors, which will make it cheaper. A yoga class is a good way to meet locals, too.

59

40. CLIMB THE WALLS

There are a couple of popular indoor rock-climbing centres in Brisbane. Or you can go rock-climbing on real rocks at Kangaroo Point cliffs. It's a popular place for budding local rock-climbers, as they build their skills to venture into the rocky playgrounds of south-east Queensland.

One of the great things about Kangaroo Point is that there are climbs of different grades. If you're there, combine the activity with kayaking—there are kayaks for hire a little further along the river towards the Story Bridge—or a picnic or barbecue. Brisbane City Council provides free barbecues. From here, you can walk to South Bank, or continue under the cliffs and further to the park under the Story Bridge.

41. SWIM AT THE OLDEST POOL IN THE SOUTHERN HEMISPHERE

The Spring Hill Baths opened in 1886. This pool is said to the oldest in-ground swimming pool still operating in the southern hemisphere. It's picture-postcard cute and, being so old, is pre-metric—it's 25 yards long. The pool is surrounded by wooden changing cubicles with brightly painted doors, and there's an upstairs grandstand. It's roofed, which makes it a good choice for swimming in summer. I used to swim laps here when I had an office job nearby. Check the Brisbane City Council website for opening hours and entry costs.

CULTURE, FROM HIGHBROW TO THE STREET

42. ENJOY SOME ART

The art gallery (museum) scene in Brisbane is dominated by the state-run Queensland Art Gallery (QAG) and Gallery of Modern Art (GOMA). They usually have some free exhibitions, as well as paid ones. The Aboriginal and Torres Strait Islander collection at QAG is well worth a visit; the exhibition changes from time to time, but there is always wonderful work to see. There are also exhibitions of Australian colonial and federation art, which are worth checking out to help give you a historical context for contemporary Queensland culture. GOMA also has a number of free displays. Both galleries also host paid exhibitions.

If you're around at the right time, another free exhibition worth checking out is the Asia–Pacific Triennial, staged at GOMA every three years for about five months. It is an eclectic showcase of contemporary art, often provocative, from Australia and our neighbours.

If you like art, there are plenty of small galleries that are worth checking out, too. Try the Webb Centre Gallery or the Project Gallery, both at the South Bank campus of Queensland College of Art. They feature lots of up-and-coming artists, so you'll see something completely different to what's on show at the large galleries. There are also several private galleries in New Farm and Fortitude Valley.

43. STREET ART BECOMES MAINSTREAM

It's hard to believe that these days the city authorities embrace street art. Not so long ago, they fought an ongoing battle against the artists and their work, sending out teams to paint out graffitied walls, or covering walls in an anti-graffiti coating. But the artists won! These days, street artists are paid to brighten drab walls of concrete. Brisbane City Council commissions the painting of walls, pillars, and bridges; it also commissions people, not just artists, to paint traffic-signal boxes. There's also a community-run street art festival, which is used to raise money to support the homeless. Hotspots are in the streets of Fortitude Valley and West End, but art is dotted all over Brisbane, so search online for addresses of new work.

44. GO TO THE LIBRARY

The State Library of Queensland (SLQ) is a great place to browse, especially if you're in Brisbane in summer and the humidity is getting to you. The best reading spaces look over the river, which is framed by trees outside the library's picture windows. Get there early, as positions go fast. The library often has small exhibitions, many of which are free. (One of my favourites is when they put on exhibitions of artists' books.)

If you're travelling with kids, there is a great children's play area on the ground floor, and librarians lead activities such as nursery rhyme singalongs and storytelling. Look online, or ask the librarians. Some branches of the Brisbane City Council library offer singalongs for young children, too.

45. GO TO THE EKKA

August is Ekka time, and Brisbanites and rural Queenslanders flock there in our thousands—so there is no way you can't rub shoulders with locals! The Ekka's formal name is the Royal Queensland Show, but no-one calls it that. It's been showcasing the best of Queensland agriculture since 1876. As well as competitions for 'best of' in agriculture, vegetable growing, cooking, and animal breeding, there are carnival rides (in Sideshow Alley) and heaps of other entertainment. The weird and wacky fowls that people have bred are something to behold, and it's a treat to watch the skill of the competitors in the woodchopping events. Agricultural shows occur all over the country. Most rural communities have small shows, and competition winners in events at these ones go on to compete in a regional round; the winners there enter the state finals, which are the competition program of the Ekka.

46. CINEMATHEQUE

Catch a free movie at the Cinematheque at GOMA. The film and video program, which focuses on retrospectives, is advertised on QAGOMA's website. You're not likely to see the movies being screened here anywhere else in Brisbane.

ENTERTAINMENT

47. GET BOARD

Into old-school arcade games and board games? Even if you're not, check out two inner-city favourites. Netherworld has scores of board games and 1970s and 80s arcade, pinball and console games to choose from. Luckily, it also has a bar and a diner to keep you refreshed while you relive your youth, or find out why your parents go on about how much fun they had way back then. Pincadia is the equivalent on the south side of the river. It's an adults-only venue, so you have to be 18 or more to get in. (Note: In June 2018, a fire in Pincadia's kitchen resulted in the business closing its doors, I hope temporarily. Check the website to see if it's re-opened.)

48. IT'S MORE THAN JUST A MOVIE AT BLUE ROOM

Blue Room Cinebar in Rosalie is a treat for movie fans. Not that you go just for the movie: you go for the whole luxurious experience. The five theatres at

Blue Room don't have many seats, but, my, are they comfortable! You get to sit in something like Gran's recliner, complete with cushions and a foot rest. You can order food and drinks from a menu at the ticket booth, and the staff will bring them to you in your seat. The food is supplied by nearby restaurants, so it's infinitely better tasting than the standard movie snacks. Tip: buy your tickets online—they're much cheaper that way.

If you want to go to the movies and support local businesses, another, slightly less glamorous option is the Cineplex cinemas at South Bank, Bulimba, Hawthorne, and Victoria Point. They are owned by a Brisbane family. These cinemas run a mix of current blockbusters and art-house movies, and are much cheaper than the multinationals.

49. EATING AS ENTERTAINMENT

Eat Street is an increasingly popular weekend outing among Brisbanites. It's a shipping-container world of tastes and live music, with more than 70 cuisines represented at different food stalls. It's great to go with a group of friends, new found or well established, or make friends with some locals there.

It's 250 metres from the Hamilton CityCat terminal, so it's easy to use public transport and enjoy a drink or two without fear of encountering police armed with alcohol breath-testers on your way home. There's a website that gives details, including upcoming events.

50. SPECIALTY BARS, FROM ROOFTOPS TO BELOW GROUND

Brisbane's balmy climate invites outdoor living— and there are plenty of rooftop bars around to help you enjoy the cool night air. Most offer views of the city lights at night, always a bonus.

There are also several specialty bars, including some underground. Whether it's the craft beer scene, the cocktail of the moment, enough whiskies to entice a Scottish aficionado across the world, or themed bars, and glamour, grunge or cutting edge, there is enough variety dotted around the city that you're sure to find several to your taste and budget.

BONUS 1. CHILL OUT WITH SOME FREE LIVE MUSIC

For a mellow take on live music, chill out at Green Jam, at the Melbourne Street Green (Queensland Performing Arts Centre) on Friday evenings. The music is laid back, and is provided by students from the Queensland Conservatorium and other music schools. Another option is hangin' with your friends at Stokehouse, at the southern end of South Bank, to enjoy a picnic on the grassy bank above the river while you take in the free music.

BONUS 2. ALL THAT JAZZ

A night out at the Brisbane Jazz Club is a visual and aural treat. The club puts on a program of wide-ranging jazz styles. It is run by volunteers, who have always been enthusiastically welcoming when I've been there. The clubhouse has a deck on the waterfront, from where you have views of the lights of the city high rises reflected in the water. Make the most of the treat, and go there on the CityHopper. The Holman Street stop is next to the jazz club.

BONUS 3. ENJOY THE ENERGY OF BRISBANE'S FLOURISHING LIVE MUSIC SCENE

In the past 30 years, the Brisbane music scene has blossomed. Brisbanites and the live-music venues support diverse local talent of many flavours. There are plenty of online resources for finding live music. However, I can't resist mentioning a few of my favourite venues. The oldest one of these is The Zoo, which, when I came to Brisbane eons ago, was one of only a handful of small venues that supported quality local music. The Tivoli has been around for a while, too. It has a theatrical but intimate vibe, and attracts some great performers. The Triffid is a great home-grown venue, not just because it's Brissie through and through, but also because its owner is John Collins, who was the bassist in one of Australia's most successful rock bands, Powderfinger.

After the gig, finish the night off at one of the many late night (or early daybreak!) party pubs, clubs and bars in Fortitude Valley. You'll need ID to get into these places after midnight. The State Government introduced this measure in the wake of a spate of alcohol- and drug-fuelled violence inside and near nightspots. You may not like it—but without ID

69

you won't get into places in what is dubbed safe-night precincts.

And when the sun comes up … you'll be ready for coffee, food, and another day out in balmy Brisbane.

TOP REASONS TO BOOK THIS TRIP

Climate: Balmy weather year-round makes for a wonderful outdoor lifestyle, whatever you're doing.

Friendliness: Big-city features combine with small-city friendliness.

Parks: All kinds, from manicured to native forest, accessible in most suburbs and with public transport.

BONUS BOOK

50 THINGS TO KNOW ABOUT PACKING LIGHT FOR TRAVEL

PACK THE RIGHT WAY EVERY TIME

AUTHOR: MANIDIPA BHATTACHARYYA

Edited by Melanie Howthorne

ABOUT THE AUTHOR

Manidipa Bhattacharyya is a creative writer and editor, with an education in English literature and Linguistics. After working in the IT industry for seven long years she decided to call it quits and follow her heart instead. Manidipa has been ghost writing, editing, proof reading and doing secondary research services for many story tellers and article writers for about three years. She stays in Kolkata, India with her husband and a busy two year old. In her own time Manidipa enjoys travelling, photography and writing flash fiction.

Manidipa believes in travelling light and never carries anything that she couldn't haul herself on a trip. However, travelling with her child changed the scenario. She seemed to carry the entire world with her for the baby on the first two trips. But good sense prevailed and she is again working her way to becoming a light traveler, this time with a kid.

INTRODUCTION

He who would travel happily
must travel light.

-Antoine de Saint-Exupéry

Travel takes you to different places from seas and mountains to deserts and much more. In your travels you get to interact with different people and their cultures. You will, however, enjoy the sights and interact positively with these new people even more, if you are travelling light.

When you travel light your mind can be free from worry about your belongings. You do not have to spend precious vacation time waiting for your luggage to arrive after a long flight. There is be no chance of your bags going missing and the best part is that you need not pay a fee for checked baggage.

People who have mastered this art of packing light will root for you to take only one carry-on, wherever you go. However, many people can find it really hard to pack light. More so if you are travelling with children. Differentiating between "must have" and "just in case" items is the starting point. There will be ample shopping avenues at your destination which are just waiting to be explored.

This book will show you 'packing' in a new 'light' – pun intended – and help you to embrace light packing practices for all of your future travels.

Off to packing!

DEDICATION

I dedicate this book to all the travel buffs that I know, who have given me great insights into the contents of their backpacks.

THE RIGHT TRAVEL GEAR

1. CHOOSE YOUR TRAVEL GEAR CAREFULLY

While selecting your travel gear, pick items that are light weight, durable and most importantly, easy to carry. There are cases with wheels so you can drag them along – these are usually on the heavy side because of the trolley. Alternatively a backpack that you can carry comfortably on your back, or even a duffel bag that you can carry easily by hand or sling across your body are also great options. Whatever you choose, one thing to keep in mind is that the luggage itself should not weigh a ton, this will give you the flexibility to bring along one extra pair of shoes if you so desire.

2. CARRY THE MINIMUM NUMBER OF BAGS

Selecting light weight luggage is not everything. You need to restrict the number of bags you carry as well. One carry-on size bag is ideal for light travel. Most carriers allow one cabin baggage plus one purse, handbag or camera bag as long as it slides under the seat in front. So technically, you can carry two items of luggage without checking them in.

3. PACK ONE EXTRA BAG

Always pack one extra empty bag along with your essential items. This could be a very light weight duffel bag or even a sturdy tote bag which takes up minimal space. In the event that you end up buying a lot of souvenirs, you already have a handy bag to stuff all that into and do not have to spend time hunting for an appropriate bag.

I'm very strict with my packing and have everything in its right place. I never change a rule. I hardly use anything in the hotel room. I wheel my own wardrobe in and that's it.

Charlie Watts

CLOTHES & ACCESSORIES

4. PLAN AHEAD

Figure out in advance what you plan to do on your trip. That will help you to pick that one dress you need for the occasion. If you are going to attend a wedding then you have to carry formal wear. If not, you can ditch the gown for something lighter that will be comfortable during long walks or on the beach.

5. WEAR THAT JACKET

Remember that wearing items will not add extra luggage for your air travel. So wear that bulky jacket that you plan to carry for your trip. This saves space and can also help keep you warm during the chilly flight.

6. MIX AND MATCH

Carry clothes that can be interchangeably used to reinvent your look. Find one top that goes well with a couple of pairs of pants or skirts. Use tops, shirts and jackets wisely along with other accessories like a scarf or a stole to create a new look.

7. CHOOSE YOUR FABRIC WISELY

Stuffing clothes in cramped bags definitely takes its toll which results in wrinkles. It is best to carry wrinkle free, synthetic clothes or merino tops. This will eliminate the need for that small iron you usually bring along.

8. DITCH CLOTHES PACK UNDERWEAR

Pack more underwear and socks. These are the things that will give you a fresh feel even if you do not get a chance to wear fresh clothes. Moreover these are easy to wash and can be dried inside the hotel room itself.

9. CHOOSE DARK OVER LIGHT

While picking your clothes choose dark coloured ones. They are easy to colour coordinate and can last longer before needing a wash. Accidental food spills and dirt from the road are less visible on darker clothes.

10. WEAR YOUR JEANS

Take only one pair of Jeans with you, which you should wear on the flight. Remember to pick a pair that can be worn for sightseeing trips and is equally eloquent for dinner. You can add variety by adding light weight cargoes and chinos.

11. CARRY SMART ACCESSORIES

The right accessory can give you a fresh look even with the same old dress. An intelligent neck-piece, a couple of bright scarves, stoles or a sarong can be used in a number of ways to add variety to your clothing. These light weight beauties can double up as a nursing cover, a light blanket, beach wear, a modesty cover for visiting places of worship, and also makes for an enthralling game of peek-a-boo.

12. LEARN TO FOLD YOUR GARMENTS

Seasoned travellers all swear by rolling their clothes for compact and wrinkle free packing. Bundle packing, where you roll the clothes around a central object as if tying it up, is also a popular method of compact and wrinkle free packing. Stacking folded clothes one on top of another is a big no-no as it makes creases extreme and they are difficult to get rid of without ironing.

13. WASH YOUR DIRTY LAUNDRY

One of the ways to avoid carrying loads of clothes is to wash the clothes you carry. At some places you might get to use the laundry services or a Laundromat but if you are in a pinch, best solution is to wash them yourself. If that is the plan then carrying quick drying clothes is highly recommended, which most often also happen to be the wrinkle free variety.

14. LEAVE THOSE TOWELS BEHIND

Regular towels take up a lot of space, are heavy and take ages to dry out. If you are staying at hotels they will provide you with towels anyway. If you are travelling to a remote place, where the availability of towels look doubtful, carry a light weight travel towel of viscose material to do the job.

15. USE A COMPRESSION BAG

Compression bags are getting lots of recommendation now days from regular travellers. These are useful for saving space in your luggage when you have to pack bulky dresses. While packing for the return trip, get help from the hotel staff to arrange a vacuum cleaner.

FOOTWEAR

16. PUT ON YOUR HIKING BOOTS

If you have plans to go hiking or trekking during your trip, you will need those bulky hiking boots. The best way to carry them is to wear them on flight to save space and luggage weight. You can remove the boots once inside and be comfortable in your socks.

17. PICKING THE RIGHT SHOES

Shoes are often the bulkiest items, along with being the dainty if you are a female. They need care and take up a lot of space in your luggage. It is advisable therefore to pick shoes very carefully. If you plan to do a lot of walking and site seeing, then wearing a pair of comfortable walking shoes are a must. For more formal occasions you can carry durable, light weight flats which will not take up much space.

18. STUFF SHOES

If you happen to pack a pair of shoes, ensure you utilize their hollow insides. Tuck small items like rolled up socks or belts to save space. They will also be easy to find.

TOILETRIES

19. STASHING TOILETRIES

Carry only absolute necessities. Airline rules dictate that for one carry-on bag, liquids and gels must be in 3.4 ounce (100ml) bottles or less, and must be packed in a one quart zip-lock bag. If you are planning to stay in a hotel, the basic things will be provided for you. It's best is to buy the rest from the local market at your destination.

20. TAKE ALONG TAMPONS

Tampons are a hard to find item in a lot of countries. Figure out how many you need and pack accordingly. For longer stays you can buy them online and have them delivered to where you are staying.

21. GET PAMPERED BEFORE YOU TRAVEL

Some avid travellers suggest getting a pedicure and manicure just the day before travelling. This not only gives you a well kept look, you also save the trouble of packing nail polish. Remember, every little bit of weight reduced adds up.

ELECTRONICS
22. LUGGING ALONG ELECTRONICS

Electronics have a large role to play in our lives today. Most of us cannot imagine our lives away from our phones, laptops or tablets. However while travelling, one must consider the amount of weight these electronics add to our luggage. Thankfully smart phones come along with all the essentials tools like a camera, email access, picture editing tools and more. They are smart to the point of eliminating the need to carry multiple gadgets. Choose a smart phone that suits all your requirements and travel with the world in your palms or pocket.

23. REDUCE THE NUMBER OF CHARGERS

If you do travel with multiple electronic devices, you will have to bear the additional burden of carrying all their chargers too. Check if a single charger can be used for multiple devices. You might also consider investing in a pocket charger. These small devices support multiple devices while keeping you charged on the go.

24. TRAVEL FRIENDLY APPS

Along with smart phones come numerous apps, which are immensely helpful in our travels. You name it and you have an app for it at hand – take pictures, sharing with friends and family, torch to light dark roads, maps, checking flight/train times, find hotels and many other things. Use these smart alternatives to traditional items like books to eliminate weight and save space.

I get ideas about what's essential when packing my suitcase.

-Diane von Furstenberg

TRAVELLING WITH KIDS

25. BRING ALONG THE STROLLER

Kids might enjoy walking for a while but they soon tire out and a stroller is the just the right thing for them to rest in while you continue your tour. Strollers also double duty as a luggage carrier and shopping bag holder. Remember to pick a light weight, easy to handle brand of stroller. Better yet, find out in advance if you can rent a stroller at your destination.

26. BRING ONLY ENOUGH DIAPERS FOR YOUR TRIP

Diapers take up a lot of space and add to the weight of your luggage. Therefore it is advisable to carry just enough diapers to last through the trip and a few for afterwards, till you buy fresh stock at your destination. Unless of course you are travelling to a really remote area, in which case you have no choice but to carry the load. Otherwise diapers are something you will find pretty easily.

27. TAKE ONLY A COUPLE OF TOYS

Children are easily attracted by new things in their environment. While travelling they will find numerous 'new' objects to scrutinize and play with. Packing just one favorite toy is enough, or if there is no favorite toy leave out all of them in favor of stories or imaginary games.

28. CARRY KID FRIENDLY SNACKS

Create a small snack counter in your bag to store away quick bites for those sudden hunger pangs. Depending on the child's age this could include chocolates, raisins, dry fruits, granola bars or biscuits. Also keep a bottle of water handy for your little one.

These things do not add much weight and can be adjusted in a handbag or knapsack.

29. GAMES TO CARRY

Create some travel specific, imaginary games if you have slightly grown up children, like spot the attractions. Keep a coloring book and colors handy for in-flight or hotel time. Apps on your smart phone can keep the children engaged with cartoons and story books. Older children are often entertained by games available on phones or tablets. This cuts the weight of luggage down while keeping the kids entertained.

30. LET THE KIDS CARRY THEIR LOAD

A good thing is to start early sharing of responsibilities. Let your child pick a bag of his or her choice and pack it themselves. Keep tabs on what they are stuffing in their bags by asking if they will be using that item on the trip. It could start out being just an entertainment bag initially but with growing years they will learn to sort the useful from the superfluous. Children as little as four can maneuver a small trolley suitcase like a pro- their experience in pull along toys credit. If you are worried that you may be pulling it for them, you may want to start with a backpack.

31. DECIDE ON LOCATION FOR CHILDREN TO SLEEP

While on a trip you might not always get a crib at your destination, and carrying one will make life all the more difficult. Instead call ahead to see if there are any cribs or roll out beds for children. You may even put blankets on the floor. Weave them a story about camping and they will gladly sleep without any trouble.

32. GET BABY PRODUCTS DELIVERED AT YOUR DESTINATION

If you are absolutely paranoid about not getting your favourite variety of diaper or brand of baby food, check out online stores like amazon.com for services in your destination city. You can buy things online ahead of your travel and get them delivered to your hotel upon arrival.

33. FEEDING NEEDS OF YOUR INFANTS

If you are travelling with a breastfed infant, you save the trouble of carrying bottles and bottle sanitization kits. For special food, or medications, you may need to call ahead to make sure you have a refrigerator where you are staying.

34. FEEDING NEEDS OF YOUR TODDLER

With the progression from infancy to toddler, their dietary requirements too evolve. You will have to pack some snacks for travelling time. Fresh fruits and vegetables can be purchased at your destination. Most of the cities you travel to in whichever part of the world, will have baby food products and formulas, available at the local drug-store or the supermarket.

35. PICKING CLOTHES FOR YOUR BABY

Contrary to popular belief, babies can do without many changes of clothes. At the most pack 2 outfits per day. Pack mix and match type clothes for your little one as well. Pick things which are comfortable to wear and quick to dry.

36. SELECTING SHOES FOR YOUR BABY

Like outfits, kids can make do with two pairs of comfortable shoes. If you can get some water resistant shoes it will be best. To expedite drying wet shoes, you can stuff newspaper in them then wrap

them with newspaper and leave them to dry
overnight.

37. KEEP ONE CHANGE OF CLOTHES HANDY

Travelling with kids can be tricky. Keep a change of
clothes for the kids and mum handy in your purse or
tote bag. This takes a bit of space in your hand
luggage but comes extremely handy in case there are
any accidents or spills.

38. LEAVE BEHIND BABY ACCESSORIES

Baby accessories like their bed, bath tub, car seat, crib
etc. should be left at home. Many hotels provide a
crib on request, while car seats can be borrowed from
friends or rented. Babies can be given a bath in the
hotel sink or even in the adult bath tub with a little bit
of water. If you bring a few bath toys, they can be
used in the bath, pool, and out of water. They can also
be sanitized easily in the sink.

39. CARRY A SMALL LOAD OF PLASTIC BAGS

With children around there are chances of a number
of soiled clothes and diapers. These plastic bags help
to sort the dirt from the clean inside your big bag.

These are very light weight and come in handy to other carry stuff as well at times.

PACK WITH A PURPOSE

40. PACKING FOR BUSINESS TRIPS

One neutral-colored suit should suffice. It can be paired with different shirts, ties and accessories for different occasions. One pair of black suit pants could be worn with a matching jacket for the office or with a snazzy top for dinner.

41. PACKING FOR A CRUISE

Most cruises have formal dinners, and that formal dress usually takes up a lot of space. However you might find a tuxedo to rent. For women, a short black dress with multiple accessory options will do the trick.

42. PACKING FOR A LONG TRIP OVER DIFFERENT CLIMATES

The secret packing mantra for travel over multiple climates is layering. Layering traps air around your body creating insulation against the cold. The same light t-shirt that is comfortable in a warmer climate can be the innermost layer in a colder climate.

REDUCE SOME MORE WEIGHT

43. LEAVE PRECIOUS THINGS AT HOME

Things that you would hate to lose or get damaged leave them at home. Precious jewelry, expensive gadgets or dresses, could be anything. You will not require these on your trip. Leave them at home and spare the load on your mind.

44. SEND SOUVENIRS BY MAIL

If you have spent all your money on purchasing souvenirs, carrying them back in the same bag that you brought along would be difficult. Either pack everything in another bag and check it in the airport or get everything shipped to your home. Use an international carrier for a secure transit, but this could be more expensive than the checking fees at the airport.

45. AVOID CARRYING BOOKS

Books equal to weight. There are many reading apps which you can download on your smart phone or tab.

Plus there are gadgets like Kindle and Nook that are thinner and lighter alternatives to your regular book.

CHECK, GET, SET, CHECK AGAIN

46. STRATEGIZE BEFORE PACKING

Create a travel list and prepare all that you think you need to carry along. Keep everything on your bed or floor before packing and then think through once again – do I really need that? Any item that meets this question can be avoided. Remove whatever you don't really need and pack the rest.

47. TEST YOUR LUGGAGE

Once you have fully packed for the trip take a test trip with your luggage. Take your bags and go to town for window shopping for an hour. If you enjoy your hour long trip it is good to go, if not, go home and reduce the load some more. Repeat this test till you hit the right weight.

48. ADD A ROLL OF DUCT TAPE

You might wonder why, when this book has been talking about reducing stuff, we're suddenly asking you to pack something totally unusual. This is because when you have limited supplies, duct tape is immensely helpful for small repairs – a broken bag, leaking zip-lock bag, broken sunglasses, you name it and duct tape can fix it, temporarily.

49. LIST OF ESSENTIAL ITEMS

Even though the emphasis is on packing light, there are things which have to be carried for any trip. Here is our list of essentials:

- Passport/Visa or any other ID

- Any other paper work that might be required on a trip like permits, hotel reservation confirmations etc.

- Medicines – all your prescription medicines and emergency kit, especially if you are travelling with children

- Medical or vaccination records

- Money in foreign currency if travelling to a different country

- Tickets- Email or Message them to your phone

50. MAKE THE MOST OF YOUR TRIP

Wherever you are going, whatever you hope to do we encourage you to embrace it whole-heartedly. Take in the scenery, the culture and above all, enjoy your time away from home.

On a long journey even a straw weighs heavy.

-Spanish Proverb

PACKING AND PLANNING TIPS

A Week before Leaving

- Arrange for someone to take care of pets and water plants

- Stop mail and newspaper

- Notify Credit Card companies where you are going.

- Change your thermostat settings

- Car inspected, oil is changed, and tires have the correct pressure.

- Passports and id is up to date.

- Pay bills.

- Copy important items and download travel Apps.

- Start collecting small bills for tips

Right Before Leaving

- Clean out refrigerator.

- Empty garbage cans.

- Lock windows.

- Make sure you have the right ID with you.

- Bring cash for tips.

- Remember travel documents.

- Lock door behind you.

- Remember wallet.

- Unplug items in house and pack chargers.

>TOURIST

READ OTHER
GREATER THAN A TOURIST
BOOKS

Greater Than a Tourist San Miguel de Allende Guanajuato Mexico:
50 Travel Tips from a Local by Tom Peterson

Greater Than a Tourist – Lake George Area New York USA:
 50 Travel Tips from a Local by Janine Hirschklau

Greater Than a Tourist – Monterey California United States:
50 Travel Tips from a Local by Katie Begley

 Greater Than a Tourist – Chanai Crete Greece:
50 Travel Tips from a Local by Dimitra Papagrigoraki

Greater Than a Tourist – The Garden Route Western Cape Province
South Africa:
50 Travel Tips from a Local by Li-Anne McGregor van Aardt

Greater Than a Tourist – Sevilla Andalusia Spain:
50 Travel Tips from a Local by Gabi Gazon

Greater Than a Tourist – Kota Bharu Kelantan Malaysia:
50 Travel Tips from a Local by Aditi Shukla

Children's Book: Charlie the Cavalier Travels the World by Lisa
Rusczyk

\>TOURIST

> TOURIST

Visit Greater Than a Tourist for Free Travel Tips
http://GreaterThanATourist.com

Sign up for the Greater Than a Tourist Newsletter for discount days, new books, and travel information:
http://eepurl.com/cxspyf

Follow us on Facebook for tips, images, and ideas:
https://www.facebook.com/GreaterThanATourist

Follow us on Pinterest for travel tips and ideas:
http://pinterest.com/GreaterThanATourist

Follow us on Instagram for beautiful travel images:
http://Instagram.com/GreaterThanATourist

> TOURIST

Please leave your honest review of this book on Amazon and Goodreads. Please send your feedback to GreaterThanaTourist@gmail.com as we continue to improve the series. Thank you. We appreciate your positive and constructive feedback. Thank you.

METRIC CONVERSIONS

TEMPERATURE

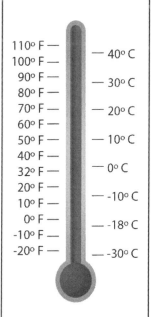

110° F —
100° F —
90° F —
80° F —
70° F —
60° F —
50° F —
40° F —
32° F —
20° F —
10° F —
0° F —
-10° F —
-20° F —

— 40° C
— 30° C
— 20° C
— 10° C
— 0° C
— -10° C
— -18° C
— -30° C

To convert F to C:

Subtract 32, and then multiply
by 5/9 or .5555.

To Convert C to F:

Multiply by 1.8
and then add 32.

32F = 0C

LIQUID VOLUME

To Convert:..................Multiply by
U.S. Gallons to Liters................. 3.8
U.S. Liters to Gallons 26
Imperial Gallons to U.S. Gallons 1.2
Imperial Gallons to Liters....... 4.55
Liters to Imperial Gallons 22
1 Liter = .26 U.S. Gallon
1 U.S. Gallon = 3.8 Liters

DISTANCE

To convert ....Multiply by
Inches to Centimeters 2.54
Centimeters to Inches 39
Feet to Meters...................... .3
Meters to Feet 3.28
Yards to Meters 91
Meters to Yards 1.09
Miles to Kilometers 1.61
Kilometers to Miles............. .62
1 Mile = 1.6 km
1 km = .62 Miles

WEIGHT

1 Ounce = .28 Grams
1 Pound = .4555 Kilograms
1 Gram = .04 Ounce
1 Kilogram = 2.2 Pounds

TRAVEL QUESTIONS

- Do you bring presents home to family or friends after a vacation?

- Do you get motion sick?

- Do you have a favorite billboard?

- Do you know what to do if there is a flat tire?

- Do you like a sun roof open?

- Do you like to eat in the car?

- Do you like to wear sun glasses in the car?

- Do you like toppings on your ice cream?

- Do you use public bathrooms?

- Did you bring your cell phone and does it have power?

- Do you have a form of identification with you?

- Have you ever been pulled over by a cop?

- Have you ever given money to a stranger on a road trip?

- Have you ever taken a road trip with animals?

- Have you ever went on a vacation alone?

- Have you ever run out of gas?

- If you could move to any place in the world, where would it be?

- If you could travel anywhere in the world, where would you travel?

- If you could travel in any vehicle, which one would it be?

- If you had three things to wish for from a magic genie, what would they be?

- If you have a driver's license, how many times did it take you to pass the test?

- What are you the most afraid of on vacation?

- What do you want to get away from the most when you are on vacation?

- What foods smells bad to you?

- What item to you bring on ever trip with you away from home?

- What makes you sleepy?

- What song would you love to hear on the radio when you're cruising on the highway?

- What travel job would you want the least?

- What will you miss most while you are away from home?

- What is something you always wanted to try?

- What is the best road side attraction that you ever saw?

- What is the farthest distance you ever biked?

- What is the farthest distance you ever walked?

- What is the weirdest thing you needed to buy while on vacation?

- What is your favorite candy?

- What is your favorite color car?

- What is your favorite family vacation?

- What is your favorite food in the world?

- What is your favorite gas station drink or food?

- What is your favorite license plate design?

- What is your favorite restaurant in the world?

- What is your favorite smell?

- What is your favorite song?

- What is your favorite sound that nature makes?

- What is your favorite thing to bring home from a vacation?

- What is your favorite vacation with friends?

- What is your favorite way to relax?

- What is your favorite weather conditions while driving?

- Where in the world would you rather never get to travel?

- Where is the farthest place you ever traveled in a car?

- Where is the farthest place you ever went North, South, East and West?

- Where is your favorite place in the world?

- Who is your favorite singer?

- Who taught you how to drive?

- Who will you miss the most while you are away?

- Who if the first person you will call when you get to your destination?

- Who brought you on your first vacation?

- Who likes to travel the most in your life?

- Would you rather be hot or cold?

- Would you rather drive above, below, or at the speed limited?

- Would you rather drive on a highway or a back road?

- Would you rather go on a train or a boat?

- Would you rather go to the beach or the woods?

TRAVEL BUCKET LIST

NOTES

Printed in Great Britain
by Amazon

36625084R00073